ACKNOWLEDGMENTS

Wm. Glasser, MD founded Reality Therapy, a system of therapy, counseling, and communication that has helped thousands of people put and keep themselves "together". This book is based on his work and is an attempt to apply the principles of Reality Therapy in yet another way. To William Glasser and to Naomi Glasser, friends always AD MULTOS ANNOS.

A SET OF DIRECTIONS FOR PUTTING (AND KEEPING) YOURSELF TOGETHER

by

Robert E. Wubbolding

A SET OF DIRECTIONS
FOR PUTTING (and KEEPING) YOURSELF TOGETHER

Copyright 1990
By Real World Publications

All rights reserved. No part of this book may be used or reproduced by any means without written permission from the publisher.

ISBN 0-9626410-0-6

CONTENTS

		Page
1.	GETTING STARTED	1
2.	IT'S YOUR CHOICE	6
3.	MAKING EXCUSES	9
4.	WHEN YOU FEEL HURT OR PAIN	19
5.	A WORD ABOUT EACH CATEGORY	24
6.	WHAT YOU CAN DO	30
7.	WHAT ELSE YOU CAN DO	32
8.	SOME QUESTIONS	46
9.	A WORD ABOUT WANTS AND GOALS	50
10.	MAKING YOURSELF ATTRACTIVE: AIDS TO MORE EFFECTIVE RELATIONSHIPS	55
11.	A WORD ABOUT PLANNING	67
12.	THE ROLE OF FAITH	74
13.	EPILOGUE	76
14.	APPENDIX	77

A SET OF DIRECTIONS FOR PUTTING YOURSELF TOGETHER

If you ...

feel depressed.
have problems getting along with friends.
get in trouble in school.
feel suicidal.
argue excessively with your spouse.
fight with your kids.
feel rejected by a lover.
are hooked on drugs.
have headaches when things are not going well.
drink too much.
have ulcers.
get lonely.
fight with the other kids on your block.
stay in your room at home too much.
don't talk to your parents.
steal a lot.
feel upset.
destroy property.
have resentments or self-pity.
feel excessively guilty.
act crazy.
feel badly, think badly, or act badly.
get angry a lot.
are excessively moody.
have trouble sleeping.

OR . . .

    If you know anyone like this.

OR . . .

    If you live with anyone like this.

OR . . .

    If you work with anyone like this.

OR . . .

    If you counsel anyone like this.

THEN . . .

    THIS BOOK IS FOR YOU ! ! !

INTRODUCTION

Being happy or "putting yourself together" is a do-it-yourself project. This book is designed to help you get started on the road to the following:

1. Feeling better.
2. Becoming happier.
3. Getting along better with other people.
4. Having your needs met more effectively.
5. Increasing your self-esteem.

It provides simple but serious suggestions for getting started. It is not intended to replace psychological counseling for those who seek it. Indeed, many people would do well to get some "outside help". But even when this decision is made to consult with a professional person, you will benefit from <u>A Set of Directions</u>... if you are willing to commit yourself to the process.

And so, whether you use this book in conjunction with another person or on your own, I have assumed that you have within you the ability to take action, to improve on your present situation, and to feel better. What you need to get started is <u>A Set of Directions for Putting (and Keeping) Yourself Together</u>.

CHAPTER I

GETTING STARTED

You can read this book quickly. It has been written that way intentionally.

The words of the book are understandable to most people. And so I have shunned the use of technical vocabulary even though the ideas are based on solid psychological theory and extensive practice by many people. It is my belief that "putting yourself together", dealing with the issues described on page i, or changing your life for the better, is a do-it-yourself project.

Nevertheless, it is possible that many readers will want to seek professional counseling. Even though we can change our lives through sustained effort by using this book or other written sources, still, many people would do well to seek out a trained person for additional help. This book can be used while receiving help from a counselor, or it can be used by a person who wants to use it alone. But it should not be viewed as a cure-all or a substitute for person-to-person therapy. After all, the fact that we can get medication over the counter does not negate the need for an occasional visit to the family physician.

HOW TO USE THIS BOOK:

<u>A Set of Directions</u>...Should not be read once and put on a shelf. It is written as a manual, a workbook. When you are finished, it should be dog-eared, written in and marked up with your own personal plans, suggestions, hopes, dreams and inspirations.

There are blanks to be filled in and pages for your thoughts and reflections. It is designed to be read and reread and even discussed with others if you are so inclined. Therefore, it is intended to be a reminder -- that if your life is not as you want it to be, you can make it better. It is also intended to help you realize that you can have more control over how you feel. Yes, a better life is possible for you, if you are willing to take the steps described in this book.

There are several conditions required, however!!!

TO TAKE CONTROL OF YOUR LIFE MORE EFFECTIVELY YOU MUST:

1. BE WILLING TO FOLLOW THROUGH DAILY.

Change requires time - time to sit and think and time for taking action or doing some things differently than you are doing them now. Just as you cannot remove a serious virus by one pill, so too a single isolated behavior will not change one's misery. It can be a start, but true change requires a sustained effort.

2. TAKE RESPONSIBILITY FOR YOUR ACTIONS.

As you progress through this book, I hope you will use words like "I chose to do such and such" rather than "they made me do it". I do not accept the fact that you are a victim of your past behavior or early childhood conflicts, problems or an "oppressive society". If you are depressed, it is not helpful to blame forces outside yourself. Remember when you point the finger of blame at others, you have 3 fingers pointing back

-2-

at yourself. So let's not blame anyone - others or self. Rather - let's look at better choices for today.

3. WORK HARD.

Anything worthwhile is worth an effort. And, don't worry about mistakes. Steve Allen once said "if you don't make mistakes, you won't make anything".

4. WORK HARD EVEN WHEN YOU DON'T FEEL LIKE IT.

There will be days when you feel miserable, apathetic or disinterested in change. Even after you make progress toward your goal, there will be times when you revert back to old feelings and behaviors. This is normal and healthy. My advice is "keep on keeping on". These "turn-backs" are only temporary.

Also, it is natural to feel bad at times. If someone has died, if you have fallen the victim of violence, if you are in danger, it is only natural and even healthy to feel grief, resentment, or fear. But, if these feelings persist for an excessively long period of time to an intense degree, and if they interfere with your life on an on-going basis, then it is important to do something about them. By reading this far in this book, you have taken the first step.

5. GIVE YOURSELF CREDIT . . . EVEN BRAG TO YOURSELF ABOUT YOURSELF.

This is not as easy to do as it seems. It could be that you are embarrassed to take credit. How many times have you put yourself down lately even in front of others?

Please pause and think for a moment. Did it really help you to criticize yourself?

6. NEVER GIVE UP!!!!

Even though progress might be slow, almost unacceptably slow, hang in there. Even though you make resolutions and don't seem to keep them or feel that you are failing, don't give up. When Winston Churchill was an old man, he was asked to give a speech at a high school graduation. When the time came for him to speak, he shuffled up to the podium, looked out at the students and delivered his entire speech in a few words, "NEVER, NEVER, NEVER GIVE UP".

If you are willing to TRY to do the above. . . READ ON. . .

The main purpose of <u>A SET OF DIRECTIONS FOR PUTTING YOURSELF TOGETHER</u> is to provide you with a clear method of self-help. Everyone of us has experienced pain to a greater or lesser degree, on a short or long term basis. Some feel unloved, or unaccepted. Others feel like failures on the job. Many people in our society are held back by feelings of loneliness, depression, grief, resentment, hatred, and the like. Others act out in anti-social ways, performing acts of crime or thoughts and become, in popular terms, crazy. And finally, some turn to alcohol or drugs which provide artificial, momentary pleasure and escape for covering over the gnawing pain inside.

This book is written to provide at least a glimmer of hope for such people. For anyone using the ideal contained herein can gain strength and feel better. Also, a family member or friend who uses these ideas with relatives or friends can lighten their burden of pain.

Finally, professionals reading this book will find many suggestions for improving their practice of counseling or therapy as well as a well-founded theory. The method and theory are based on Reality Therapy. But don't be scared off by the word "therapy". Rather, get turned on by the word "reality". These ideas are for everyone . . . not just those who go to a therapist's office!

CHAPTER 2

IT'S YOUR CHOICE

It is within your power to feel better. This statement can be both frightening and encouraging. It is frightening because if you accept it, you can no longer blame society for your misery. If you're a student, you can no longer blame the teachers or the school or your parents if you feel upset or unhappy. If you are married, you cannot blame your spouse as the source of tension. If you are an employee, no longer can you blame the boss, the job, the traffic, the weather or 1000 other excuses which we all use to stay emotionally immobilized. More on excuses in Chapter 3.

The first statement in this chapter is also encouraging. Yes, you can feel better. But feeling enthused about life or excited about a school project, or warmed by a relationship is not the result of your effort to change other people. If you have been married more than one day, you know the futility of trying to change your spouse. Most students know that their teachers are not going to change to meet the students' desires. And rare is the employer or work supervisor who will change to meet the employees' expectations. Spouses, teachers, and employers do indeed change, but this change should not be expected until WE change first.

I wish to emphasize that you can feel better by recognizing that you can make better choices to take better control of how you live. You have within you an enormous source of power, an engine that you can start and keep running for hours on end. The first choice I would like you to make is to tell yourself now that "there is hope for me. I can feel better". To say this to yourself or aloud is a choice. Don't worry whether you are convinced of it at this time. Belief will follow later. Say it now, preferably out loud!!!

DON'T BLAME YOURSELF:

One serious mistake you might make after reading the above information is to think "if I can't blame others, then I should blame myself". Wrong! You need not blame yourself either. Don't blame others and don't blame yourself. It will serve no purpose to look for a scapegoat. Our motto here is "Let's fix the problem, let's not fix the blame".

SMALL CHANGE = BIG SAVINGS:

You might never feel totally happy or free of worries, depression, resentment, guilt or other limiting feelings and thoughts. Part of being human is to feel pain occasionally. But what if you could feel just a little better? What if you could feel 5% better? What if you could change your life for the better even a tiny amount? My belief is that, in a sense, there is no such thing as a slight change. If you raise your bodily temperature just 5%, would you know the difference? You would have a temperature of approximately 103°. This amount of fever constitutes a serious medical condition. And so a slight increase makes a huge difference. Similarly, if you change the direction of the steering wheel on your car 1/8 or 1/4 of an inch, would you know the difference? Yes, you would. Turning the steering wheel a slight amount can result in a major change of direction. The same is true of the changes you make in the way you live. The choice might seem to be a minor one. The change might be slight. But if you can maintain the new direction even a change of 5% will be noticeable and beneficial to you. But don't expect miracles. The program begun by using this book takes time and hard work.

GETTING STARTED: Reality Therapy teaches that CHOICE is at the basis of whether you have pain or pleasure in your life. Of course, few people feel better by simply saying "Today I'm going to feel good." Such statements are a start, but to make an even better start, it is necessary to DO things in order to reach the goal of feeling better. In living the ideas of Reality Therapy, you need to make small, specific choices to do positive things each day. Remember "Well begun is half done". And so, in order to begin . . . .

Write down 3 things you will do today to feel better (don't worry about how "insignificant" they might be).

1. _____

2. _____

3. _____

CHAPTER 3

DEALING WITH EXCUSES

It's quite possible that the thought of change, and even more, the thought that you can choose to change, is uncomfortable. Even as you progress and begin to change for the better, it is possible that you will look at the obstacles ahead and want to give up. But giving up and turning back will be less appealing if you now make a searching inventory of your own excuses or inner obstacles to change.

WHAT IS AN EXCUSE? An excuse is putting the reasons for failure on forces outside ourselves. Flip Wilson used to say "The devil made me do it". This is a convenient way to avoid the responsibility of saying he chose to do it. Keep in mind, we all have excuses and they serve at times to help us maintain our self-esteem.

TAKE YOUR TIME. I am not suggesting that you abruptly discard all excuses. To abandon them completely will take time. So don't rush. Remember the Irish proverb "When God made time, he made plenty of it", and so at this stage, it is useful to do three tasks:

1. Ennumerate Your Excuses.

2. Ask what purpose they serve.

3. Stop asking others for excuses.

A HELPFUL ACTIVITY: Below are 5 categories of activities. List several specific possible goals under each one. These should be your own personal desires. Then list your excuses for not attaining them. I've given

-9-

one of my favorite excuses under each category to help get you started. Remember, make this an enjoyable activity. We all have excuses. We've used them for years. Consequently, it is important to keep in mind that you won't be able to banish all excuses quickly. But after listing them on the next page, you will be less inclined to use one or the other as often as in the past. A small change in your thinking is very helpful in the long run. (Reminder: The "best" excuses are those which put the control outside of ourselves or lessen our own inner ability to choose.)

A. **INVOLVEMENT WITH PEOPLE** - This category refers to anything you do to get closer to other human beings.

Activity:	Excuse for avoiding it
Example: Developing a larger circle of friends	"My schedule won't allow for it"
1.	1.
2.	2.
3.	3.
4.	4.
5.	5.

B. **ACCOMPLISHING SOMETHING** - This category refers to doing something that results in a sense of achievement or self-esteem.

Activity:	Excuse for avoiding it
Example: Cleaning garage	"The kids will just mess it up again"
1.	1.
2.	2.
3.	3.
4.	4.
5.	5.

C. **HAVING FUN** - This category refers to doing something which you enjoy. Mark Twain said "Fun is what you do when you don't have to do it".

Activity:	Excuse for avoiding it
Example: Buying an album of my favorite comedians.	"Not enough time to get to it this week"

1.   1.

2.   2.

3.   3.

4.   4.

5.   5.

D. BEING INDEPENDENT OR FREE - This category refers to acting on your own or without excessive restraints.

Activity:	Excuse for avoiding it
Example: Procrastinating the writing of a letter.	"There's too much to do. There's not enough time."
1.	1.
2.	2.
3.	3.
4.	4.
5.	5.

E. TAKING CARE OF MY HEALTH - This category refers to getting exercise, diet, and the basics of physical hygeine.

Activity:	Excuse for avoiding it
Example: Eating a second dessert.	"It doesn't make any difference."
1.	1.
2.	2.
3.	3.
4.	4.
5.	5.

F. A WORD ABOUT THE CATEGORIES - These 5 categories relate to the 5 basic human needs that exist in all human beings. These are what drives us to do all our activities. They are like the legs of a chair, and it's important to keep them in balance.

A. BELONGING.

B. POWER OR ACHIEVEMENT.

C. FUN AND ENJOYMENT.

C. FREEDOM OR INDEPENDENCE.

E. SURVIVAL.

Most activities fulfill more than one of these needs and so some of the activities you listed above probably fit under more than one of these labels. This is perfectly O.K.

There is no point in meticulously distinguishing between each need when you discuss your activities and excuses.

GETTING STARTED IN ABANDONING EXCUSES: One way to start to lessen your own excuse making is to avoid asking others for excuses. It's ironic but if you can consistently avoid asking one other person for excuses, you will learn to make fewer of your own excuses. A good place for parents to begin is to avoid asking your own children why they are fighting or why they are late for supper.

I will now give you the reason that all children fight. After hearing this, you will never have to ask them again!! On the next page you will find the answer to the question asked by parents since the dawn of time! "Why do kids fight?" The answer is . . .

**CHILDREN FIGHT BECAUSE
THE OTHER PERSON STARTED IT!**

Rarely does the child say "I'm fighting because I hit him first" or "I'm fighting because it seemed like a good choice". If you simply ask them "How will you work out your problem" or "What's your plan now?", you will avoid their excuses and you will be less inclined to make your own excuses in the future.

SOME FINAL WORDS ABOUT EXCUSES. I would hope that you will now spend a few minutes thinking about the following principles.

1. Excuses are not bad. They serve a purpose. They protect us from feeling excessive failure.

2. Therefore, don't try to get rid of all of them at once. Start gradually and be patient with yourself.

3. Don't criticize yourself or put yourself down if you don't achieve 100% freedom from excuses overnight. To change for the better is a life-long project. "Putting yourself together" ends only in the next life.

4. Start by not asking why people around you make mistakes. When they fail at any effort, simply ask them how they will try to succeed the next time.

CHAPTER 4

WHEN YOU FEEL HURT OR PAIN

Every reader knows the feeling of failure, powerlessness, weakness, or lack of control over a portion of your life. Perhaps you have experienced a death of a loved one, a rejection by a friend or relative, failure on the job, too much work, deadlines that are impossible to meet and on and on. The feelings accompanying these assaults are well known to all of us: Hurt and Pain. There are two crucial questions surrounding hurt and pain which need to be answered. One is "How did I get there?" and more importantly "What do I intend to do about it?" The second question will be discussed later. But the first question must be answered now.

When something happens to us such as the examples above, we often cannot control our immediate reaction. When a loved one suddenly dies, we feel mourning, grief, anger, depression, guilt, and a host of other emotions. These are the only feelings available to us for a while - sometimes for a long while. But it is not necessary to live with such misery forever. If a person is depressed for an excessively long period of time, it is because he/she gave up. . .gave up on involvement with people or activities which would have provided you with at least some relief. These at first might appear to be harsh words and they are difficult to accept. Keep in mind the following points:

1. Such feelings are to be expected.

2. Such feelings are appropriate for a while.

3. It is healthy to express them within limits. Thus, it is healthy to cry when sad.

4. It is not healthy to nurse them for excessively long periods of time.

5. Such feelings can be lessened and at least partially replaced by positive feelings.

GIVING UP:

I stated above that giving up on people and activities lengthens the time that you feel upset and increases the degree of hurt or pain. Other results of giving up include getting in trouble (such as a child who is upset about the parents' divorce), pessimistic and cynical thinking, and aches and pains that many people attribute to "stress".

Even though giving up on people and activities leads to increased misery, it is absolutely useless and senseless to blame yourself, criticize yourself or put yourself down. From now on, adopt the slogan that "People (I) always try to do the best they (I) can." If you are willing to at least TRY to accept this, write it down in your own handwriting:

_____

_____

It's quite possible that in the past you "gave up" -- gave up on a relationship, a project, a hobby, etc. You remained immobilized, stared out the windows, watched TV all day, sulked around feeling sorry for yourself, thought a lot of negative thoughts about

-20-

yourself or others, asked "Why?" or moaned "If only . . . if only . . . if only . . . if only . . ." There is no need to be ashamed of this. We all do it to some extent on occasion. It is a perfectly normal choice. But the purpose of this book is to help you figure out a better way to live -- other than staring out the window, watching excessive TV, sulking, self-pitying, being down on yourself or others, asking "Why me?" or saying "If only . . ."

And so, I would like to ask you to write 3 things below that you could do when you get the urge to give up, to get excessively angry, depressed, or to get overly negative about the world around you, etc. Keep in mind the activivies need not involve a direct confrontation with the problem. For example, a form of physical exercise can help a person feel less depressed even though the cause (death of a loved one) is irreversible.

1. _____

_____

2. _____

_____

3. _____

_____

Could it be that in the past when you "gave up", you went beyond that point into an even greater degree of negativism? I would now like to provide specific categories for the negativism described earlier in this Chapter. Usually people who have given up on relationships with other people or activities that they feel good about, perform behaviors on a regular basis that fit one or more of the following types of activity:

1. NEGATIVE DOING

2. NEGATIVE OR CRAZY THINKING

3. NEGATIVE PHYSICAL ACTIVITIES (sometimes involuntary)

4. NEGATIVE FEELINGS

Below are contained several examples of each. Describe briefly how you showed the negativism in your life. Don't dwell on this however.

And, if you intend to pass this book on to someone else, use another piece of paper for your statements.

Above all, tell yourself "NOW, I WILL NOT FEEL GUILTY ABOUT PAST NEGATIVISM. I AM MERELY WRITING IT SO AS TO DISCARD IT!!"

1. Negative Doing (such as any kind of hurtful doing: (stealing, cheating, self-centeredness, etc.)

———————————————

———————————————

———————————————

2. Negative or Crazy Thinking (such as

excessive pessimism, even psychotic thinking)

___

___

3. Negative or Physical Activities (such as harmful diet, laziness, some sicknesses, e.g. digestive, back, skin problems, or anything due to "nerves")

___

___

4. Negative Feelings (such as anger, resentment, self-pity, guilt, fear, shame, regret, stress, etc.)

___

___

    Remember to choose not to feel guilty about these behaviors. Rather, you have merely identified behaviors which you have performed which were the best you could do at that time. Nevertheless, they are not the kinds of things you wish to continue, and you now have taken a major step toward discarding these unhelpful attitudes.

CHAPTER 5

A WORD ABOUT EACH CATEGORY

1. NEGATIVE DOING

Some people get involved in lying, cheating, stealing or behaviors which hurt others. Occasionally we all act "irresponsibly", paying little attention to possible consequences. If you've never gotten a speeding ticket, never said an unkind word, or never hurt yourself or anyone else, please call me immediately. I'd love to meet you. Or better, call **RIPLEY'S BELIEVE IT OR NOT!!!** There is a saying "Nobody's perfect". There is also a saying "to err is human, to forgive divine".

The reason for forgiving yourself **NOW** is that at the time you generated these behaviors, they seemed to you the best way to fulfill your needs. Cheating on an exam was a way to get a passing grade and to get a sense of achievement, accomplishment, or self-worth. Or, it was, perhaps, a way to avoid the pain of failure and thereby gain a sense of power or control.

Hurting others in words or deeds is often an attempt to gain acceptance from a peer group. It can lead to temporary popularity and a feeling of momentary belonging. Besides, it seems to be fun!

At the time you did these things, the choices seemed to be helpful. Now that you have decided to put this behavior behind you, it is to your advantage to forgive yourself. To continue to feel guilt about them will only increase the likelihood of reverting back to them.

-24-

The reason for putting them behind you is that they didn't really accomplish what you had hoped for. In short, they did not help you. If they did, you would not be reading this book. When you did them, you may have thought that they would bring about self-worth, popularity, fun, etc., but in the long range, they failed to accomplish their purpose. They may have even violated your moral code and resulted in even more intense feelings of guilt, low self-worth and pain.

And so, today is the day to do three things:

1. Admit that even though in the past you generated some negative choices (which then appeared to be good choices), still you **NOW** recognize that to continue them would not help.

2. Forgive yourself. Even though you might not "feel" that you can do this, it is important to **TRY** to forgive yourself **NOW**.

3. Decide to put these ineffective choices behind you. Remember, such a choice is not easily carried out. It takes time and relapses can be expected.

2. NEGATIVE THINKING (Pessimistic or Psychotic Thinking)

Perhaps you see the bleak side of life. We all do, occasionally, and it is perfectly normal. At times, there is much to be negative about. For it is hard to rejoice about unemployment, inflation, personal disasters and the like. And so, in speaking about "negative thinking" I am not suggesting that you ignore your environment by adopting a naive way of thinking. I am suggesting that to see only the problems and bleak side of life will not increase your happiness nor your ability to deal with the world around you. The definition of a pessimist is a man who wears both suspenders and a belt!! If your conversation is characterized by "Ain't it awful!", "I can't . . .", "Everything is unfair", Poor me", and many other similar statements, you can benefit from this book, which is designed to provide you with a "check-up from the neck up".

It will also help you avoid what one writer calls "stinkin' thinkin'" and "hardening of the attitudes".

On the other hand, your mental life might have been characterized by psychotic thinking. In this case you went to extremes, but hopefully you have received help and are now on the road to recovery. Even if you are afflicted with a serious mental disorder, you can benefit from this book if you are willing to work at the ideas and put them into practice.

There is a poem whose author is unknown:

"Two men looked out from behind bars.
One saw the mud.
The other, the stars."

3. NEGATIVE PHYSICAL ACTIVITIES

Have you ever been told that your ache or pain is due to "stress"? That it is "psychosomatic"? That it is due to "nerves"? If so, then you had a problem that could be at least partly addressed by the ideas contained in this book. Of course, whenever there is a physical problem, a physician should be consulted so that good medical practice can be followed. But some problems are caused or aggravated by our life styles and decisions. Some headaches, backaches, and other ailments, though very painful, can be lessened by following the ideas contained in this book. The choices we make influence our bodies. Many years ago, President Eisenhower's physician said that an ulcer sufferer needs to switch from being: "a heller to a what the heller".

Almost daily, we learn from the media about the connection between our health and our life style. And so, part of your plan for pulling yourself together should be closer attention to your diet, exercise, amount of sleep. This aspect of putting yourself together is not emphasized in this book because ample information is provided by other sources. And so, if you consult such resources, you will find specific dietary and other suggestions for lowering cholesterol, lessening the chance of cancer, heart disease, and other ailments. Such effective behaviors add to the goal of this book: to help you smell the daisies longer so that you don't push them up earlier!!!

4. NEGATIVE FEELINGS

Many of you have undoubtedly felt angry, depressed, lonely, resentful, etc., for a short or even a long period of time. Such feelings eat away at your insides and sap strength and energy that could be used to feel better and attain a sense of achievement in your life. There is a saying, "Resentment is an acid that eats its own container". The same is true of all the other negative feelings.

So today is a day of decision. The fundamental decision seems to be between the following two choices:

1. To nurse, nurture and nourish your negative feelings: to spend time thinking about a past event that caused you to feel guilt; to go over and over in your mind something that someone did to you; to cultivate and fertilize your hurt and resentment toward a person who treated you unfairly.

2. To cut loose these feelings and allow them to float away. Think of yourself as a ship that is towing the dead hulk of a wrecked ship. It saps your strength, lessens your energy, absorbs your attention, and prevents you from functioning at your fullest capacity.

There is really only one good choice: cut the tow line and let the feelings go. You will not overcome them by indulging them, by dredging them up and examining them again. You have probably looked at them 1000 times under your mental microscope and so another 1000 times will reveal nothing new.

Today is the day for you to begin to discard your negative feelings.

(Notice, I said **begin**. It is a life-long task. Don't worry if it is not accomplished in a day or a week!)

5. BE OPTIMISTIC

You notice I said that the above symptoms are "choices". These are not the same clear cut choices which you make when you pick out a pair of shoes or decide what tie to wear today.

-28-

But if you think of these "negative choices" as just that -- things you have chosen -- then you can make other choices -- "positive choices", strength-giving choices", "successful choices". If you have made choices in the past to do negative things, (and we all have done that!), then you can make positive choices which will result in better feelings, better health, more friends and increased happiness. In other words, you will have begun to "put yourself together".

CHAPTER 6

WHAT CAN YOU DO

This chapter is a summary of two ways to think about how to change your life, how to put yourself together, keep yourself together, and live a more rewarding and fulfilling life. For some readers, these will be new ways to think about yourself and your possibilities. For others, these three suggestions will validate what you already know.

The first idea was previewed in Chapter 5. But it deserves added emphasis. So here it is again.

MAKE A DECISION

CHOOSE

Yes, make a decision; choose to turn your life around today. "Today is the first day of the rest of your life" is a powerful philosophical statement. Just as you might have told yourself "I give up", now is the time to tell yourself:

I'LL DO IT

Today you are making a decision to turn your life around, to do better, to improve yourself.

The second step is to avoid efforts to change others -- whether it is your husband, wife, children, teachers, boss, employees, the government, etc. It might sound horrible to you to suggest not trying to change people or institutions. I am saying that the second step is one of FOCUS, EMPHASIS. This second step is

FOCUS ON SELF

Yes, focus on what you can change -- yourself. If you've been married longer than one day, you know how hard it is to change another person. Your ability to change a human being ends with the outer layer of your own skin. It is hard enough to change what you want, what you do, what you feel, what you think, or how you see things. It is impossible to "force" another person to conform to our wishes. Some people will die rather than change. History is filled with "martyrs".

Besides, the more we try to change other people to conform to our wishes, the more frustrated and unhappy we become, because when they resist, we often unwisely try harder to force a change. It is a vicious cycle leading to our own increased negative doing, negative thinking, negative feelings and even negative health.

And so, the **FOCUS** here is on **CHANGING SELF**. What can you change about yourself which would help you?

-31-

CHAPTER 7

WHAT ELSE CAN YOU DO

Earlier I hinted at action you could take to improve your life when I asked you to write 3 things you would do today. Perhaps you had a hard time writing something. The directions really weren't very exact! That was intentional. Before I describe exactly what you can do, it is important to understand that what you do to feel better should fit into 4 categories which are parallel to the negative signs of misery. The positive signs are:

1. POSITIVE DOING

2. POSITIVE AND RATIONAL THINKING

3. POSITIVE (HEALTHFUL) PHYSICAL ACTIVITY

4. POSITIVE FEELINGS

If you want to turn your life around, examine how you can build up these categories. It is as if you have 4 mental barrels to be filled, and each day you add something to at least one of the barrels.

-32-

Figure 1: Mental Barrel Number One.

When you add something to the POSITIVE DOING BARREL, you perform in two ways -- either for yourself or for others. (Many things we do, of course, are for both ourselves and for others!) Some examples of doing for yourself are reading a good book, taking a course at a school, asserting yourself in a social setting, etc. Doing for others could be smiling at people, doing a favor for someone, volunteering your help in any way, and the like. Below is a chart. write down four things which you will do today that can be put into the POSITIVE DOING BARREL. Two of them should be "for myself" and two of them "for others". (Feel free to add more than two!) Be sure to use pencil -- not ink!

FOR SELF	FOR OTHERS
1. 2. 3. 4. 5.	1. 2. 3. 4. 5.

Now examine these more carefully. Did they have the following characteristics?

1. **Controlled by you only.** If any of them depended on your husband, wife, children or anyone else, go back and change it. If you thought as you wrote it, "If so and so does this ... I'll do that ... ", go back and change it to what you will do regardless of what anyone else does.

2. **Simple.** Don't make plans too complicated. The motto is KIS: "Keep it Simple!"

3. **Specific.** If you wrote "The next time such and such happens" or "I'm going to be friendly ...", go back and make it more exact. "I will greet so and so tonight with a smile and a friendly 'hello'." Or "I will write a one-page letter to aunt so-and-so today at 10:00 A.M."

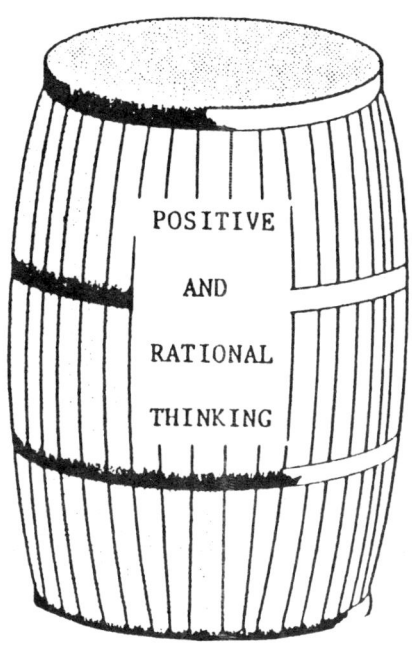

Figure 2: Mental Barrel Number 2

Adding to your second barrel, POSITIVE AND RATIONAL THINKING, consists of two exercises: A) imaging to yourself the attainment of what you want; and, B) putting positive thoughts into your mind.

> **A. Imaging:** In this technique you imagine to yourself that you already are the kind of person you want to be, or you imagine already having what you want. Spend several minutes quietly imaging this each day for 5 minutes in a quiet place. Perhaps you imagine you are a patient, kind and happy person on your job. Imagine what you would be doing. Be exact and precise -- down to the clothes you and others are wearing.

Or, imagine you have the income you desire. Where would you go? Would it be a trip to the Carribean? What would you do there? Be exact and precise and spend a specific amount of time imaging.

B. **Positive Thinking.** The best way to develop this quality is to have several personal mottos or slogans which you repeat aloud every day!

Some favorites of mine are:

1. "It's a great day to go get 'em."
2. "If it is to be, it is up to me."
3. "I'm a Winner, I'm a Winner, I'm a Winner."
4. "Yes indeed, I succeed."
5. "I can, I will. I can, I will. I can, I will."

The goal of these statements is to replace the negative thoughts which have plagued you up to now. Remember: "Today is the first day of the rest of your life." Today is the day you turned your life around.

On the next page is a chart. Write in your topics which you will imagine in your own mind and your own slogans which you will repeat each day as you get dressed to start the day!!

TOPIC	SLOGANS
1.	1.
2.	2.
3.	3.
4.	4.
5.	5.

Don't forget to make a plan to do these things at a specific time. Write down the exact time. (This time use a pen.)

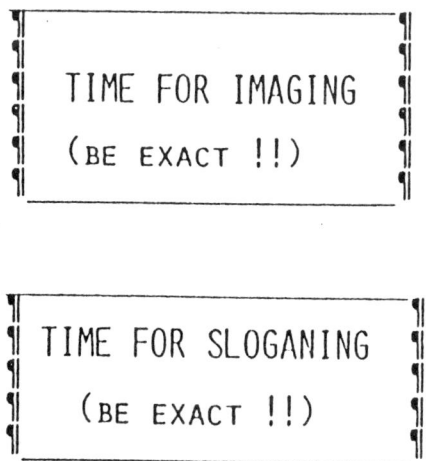

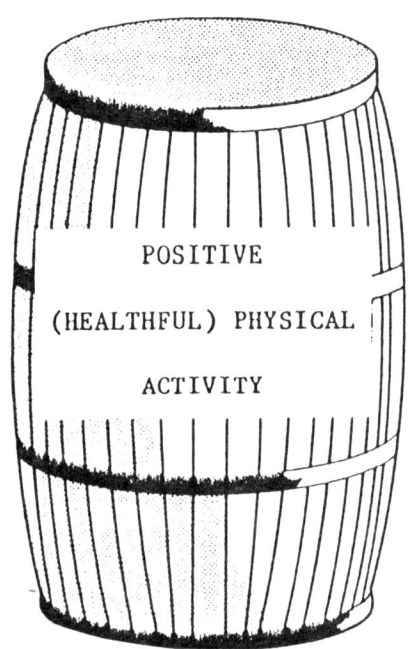

Figure 3: Mental Barrel Number 3.

Adding to your third mental barrel, POSITIVE (HEALTHFUL) PHYSICAL ACTIVITIES, consists of making plans as you did when you added to the first barrel. But in this barrel you put only physical activities. The kind of physical activities which you insert depends on your physical strength at the present. If there is some doubt as to whether you should perform a physical activity consult your physician. Thus, people who are bedridden with serious heart conditions should not attempt to run sprints!!! I wish to encourage people to build gradually on already existing strength -- not to be foolhardy!

Such physical activities could thus be very simple or very complex depending on what you are accustomed to doing!! For some people who haven't taken care of themselves, a plan to brush their teeth or take a bath or to get out of bed early might be a different and an appropriate plan. For those of you who feel more strength in your lives, a walk around the block of 5, 10, 15, or 30 minutes would be strength-giving and very appropriate. For others, more strenuous activities are necessary, e.g., racketball, etc. These activities should have several characteristics. They should be:

1. **Realistic.** Be sure what you select is attainable. If you won't walk everyday but can realistically do it every other day, make a plan to increase the activity gradually. Again, if your health demands it, consult a physician if necessary!!

2. **Measurable.** Your plan for physical activity should include answers to such questions as "What?", "When?", "Where?", and "How often?"

3. **Repetitive.** If a plan is to help you take better charge of how you feel and how you live your life, it must be performed -- NOT ONCE -- but TIME AND TIME AGAIN. To take a brisk walk once a month or once every six months will not provide the strength you desire. It should occur often, just as a champion (strong!) athlete practices day after day. Your mental and emotional strength will develop through repeated follow-throughs on your plans.

Below is a chart with a sample plan which I have formulated and which I have followed through on every day. Write down 9 more plans or as many as you can think of. These are plans which you **COULD** do! Do not yet make a firm commitment to do them!! At this stage they are only possible plans which you think could help you to gain strength. Write 9 additional plans or as many as you wish to write. The first plan serves only as an example.

Now select one of these plans and write it in the same chart on the next page following the phrase "I will. . ." Remember, the first word which you write under "MY PLAN" should be a verb. But words and phrases such as "try to. . .", "could", "might", "would like to. . ." are omitted. Phrases like "sing in the shower", "do 20 sit-ups", "take a brisk walk", are proper ways to phrase your plans.

-40-

	PLAN	WHEN	WHERE	HOW LONG	HOW OFTEN
1.	Exercise every day	7:00 A.M.	Bedroom floor	7 min.	7 days per week
2.					
3.					
4.					
5.					
6.					
7.					
8.					
9.					
10.					

MY PLAN	WHEN	WHERE	HOW LONG	HOW OFTEN
I Will				

Now copy this chart over in your own handwriting and post it where you can see it every day. A good place is on your bathroom mirror. Your final activity for adding it to your third barrel, POSITIVE (HEALTHFUL) PHYSICAL ACTIVITIES, is to tell someone that you've decided to undertake this new project. Write down the name of the person you will tell and when you will tell them.

Name of Person I will tell about my new physical activity.	What I will tell him/her.	When I will tell him/her (exact time).

The above step-by-step method might seem simple, even childish, to some. But it is an effort to help you do what you have been wanting to do and haven't had the energy to execute!! It is an effort to help you make a precise plan of action. There is a saying, "To fail to plan is a plan to fail." There is also a saying, "A journey of 1,000 miles is begun in one step." If you write down your plans, you have taken the first step.

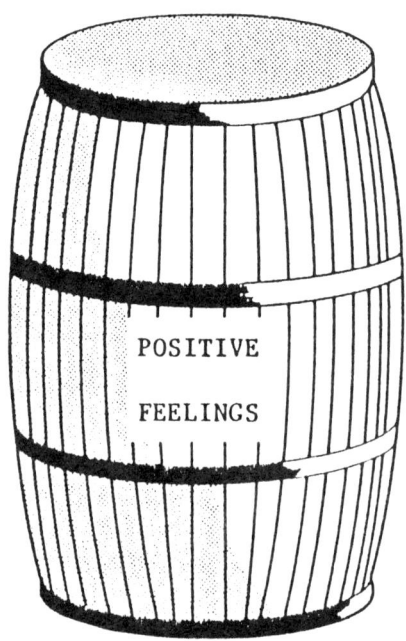

Figure 4: Mental Barrel Number 4

This barrel is in many ways the most important one. Yet you can't directly put anything into it. If you work on filling the other barrels this one will automatically be filled. If you change what you're doing (Barrel #1), improve what you are thinking (Barrel #2), and engage in regular healthful activities (Barrel #3), the payoff will be a FULL BARREL OF POSITIVE FEELINGS. If you regularly stand up for yourself, give of yourself to others, put the good and the beautiful into your mind, take care of the marvelous body wherein you reside, you will live a life of happiness, with fewer of the debilitating effects of:

SELF-PITY

GUILT

ANGER

RESENTMENT

FEAR

DEPRESSION

SHAME

HATRED

ANXIETY

Instead you will have:

SATISFACTION

PEACE OF MIND

PATIENCE

FULFILLMENT

JOY

SPIRIT OF GIVING

TRUST

HOPE

SECURITY

ACCEPTANCE

CHAPTER 8

SOME QUESTIONS

Question 1: Is it really that simple? Can I completely get rid of my negative feelings?

Answer: You will never completely get rid of negative feelings, negative behaviors or "problems". Making positive plans is a lifetime project. Happiness, consisting of the above feelings and sentiments, is not a destination.

HAPPINESS IS A JOURNEY

It requires hard work, continued planning and evaluation of how you are living your life. Fulfillment is not a photograph, a snapshot which is static and frozen.

FULFILLMENT IS A MOVING PICTURE

As a moving picture, it constantly requires watching. It requires evaluation. It requires planning. It requires doing.

Question 2: If I utilize this self improvement method, will I feel better soon?

Answer: There will be a time lag from the time you perform your strength giving activities and the time you feel better. There is a lag between when athletes exercise and the time when they "feel in shape." It will be similar when you take charge of the way you live your life. You will feel better and you will feel the difference only after a period of time. I cannot say what the exact time is. It is different for every person.

But one caution is important. YOU WILL BE TEMPTED TO GIVE UP IF YOU DON'T GET QUICK RESULTS. That is the very time to continue your sustained activity. Remember, your plans must be repetitive.

Question 3: Don't I have to resolve my past problems if I'm to really feel better on a permanent basis?

Answer: There are many people in the helping professions who would answer "yes" to this. Some feel that it is necessary to relive the past, discuss early childhood relationships, and to resolve your unconscious conflicts in order to truly put yourself together and change your life on a permanent basis.

Indeed, sometimes, it might be useful to discuss past history with someone -- a trusted friend or a professional person. If something is causing you PRESENT pain or hurt, it might be helpful to get it out in the open.

This book is based upon the principles of Reality Therapy that says that pain and hurt are due to causes that are PRESENT, not past. A past event such as abuse experienced as a child, a wartime trauma, a past rejection by a friend or spouse could be on a person's mind at the present time. Therefore, it might be useful to bring the experience up for discussion.

But to discuss past events separately and endlessly is not part of the "Set of Directions". The "Directions" discussed here are based on the principle that pain, hurt and all upsetness is the result of the past that something is missing in the person's life NOW. More specifically it is missing in the categories described earlier:

    Belonging -   Feeling that I'm alienated from others.

    Power, Achievement -   Feeling that I'm not a competent person.

    Fun, Enjoyment -   Feeling that I'm bored with life.

    Freedom, Independence - Feeling that I'm trapped, imprisoned and cannot make satisfying choices.

Question 3: Is that all I have to do. . . make plans?

Answer: NO. There are other things you can do. The most important step comes even before you make plans. I have saved the first and fundamental step till now. It is stated in two ways:

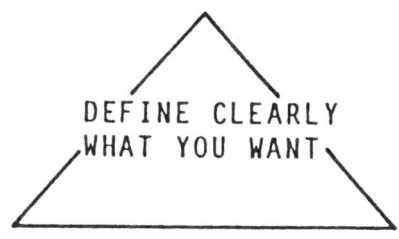

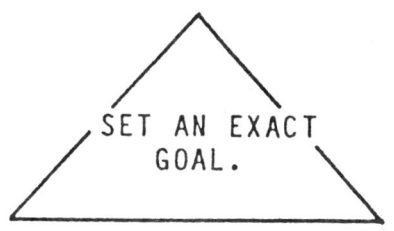

CHAPTER 9

A WORD ABOUT WANTS AND GOALS

Stated in Chapter 7 is the injunction: DEFINE CLEARLY WHAT YOU WANT. SET AN EXACT GOAL. It is crucial to decide what you want for yourself, what you want to aim at. In doing this, it is important that you do the following when you define your wants and set your goals. (By the way, I consider defining wants and setting goals as identical. And so these phrases can be used interchangeably.)

You must:

1. Categorize what you want. Put your goals into several meaningful categories.

    Personal, for example, get your weight down to a specific amount.

    Social, for example, form 3 new friendships in the next 2 months.

    Financial, for example, save "X" number of dollars in the next year, or earn "X" number of dollars in the next year.

    Physical, for example, get 1/2 hour of exercise per day.

    Intellectual, for example, read 1/2 hour per day.

    Spiritual, for example, perform one altruistic activity per day wherein you directly contribute to the welfare of another person.

2. **Write down these goals.**

   If your goals are to be achieved they must be written down. It is not enough to "keep them in my head". You are serious about them only if you commit them to paper. It helps to post them. If you want a new Cadillac, post a picture of it where you can see it. If you want a dream house, post a picture of such a house where it is visible. If you want less stress, post a picture of yourself in a relaxed pose. Read your goals 2 times a day and revise them regularly.

3. **Decide to focus your thinking and energy on them.**

   This decision will help you. As you mull over your wants and goals, do not worry how you will attain them. You will discover ways. You will make plans. But first, think about them. Focus your thinking on them. Decide to energize yourself toward attaining them. Make this decision many times each day.

4. **Be self-accepting when you fail.**

   There will be times when you feel you have failed to work toward the goal. You went off your diet, you did not do what you told yourself you would do. You did not save the money you wanted to save, you got off schedule in some way. You did something you are ashamed of, etc.

-51-

The urge will be to give up, say "what's the use?" and wallow in feelings of misery, guilt and failure.

At this time, it is important to tell yourself: "Tomorrow is another day." Review the goals again and refuse to feel negative!!!!

Remember the words of William James, the father of American psychology, who said that the greatest human discovery is that we can change our circumstances by changing our attitudes. When you fail, change the guilt and self-criticism into positive thoughts about "the next time".

5. Picture your want as already fulfilled.

Spend time every day imagining yourself as having achieved the goal. If you want to be popular, picture in your mind's eye what you would be doing. Imagine having friends and what they say to you. Picture yourself having fun -- at the beach, on the tennis court, or at a party. You have already achieved it mentally.

6. Share the goal only with people who will encourage you.

Don't share your want or goal with people who will ridicule or put you down. If you really and truly have decided that you want to be the head of a company, visualize it, discuss it. But don't reveal it to negative thinkers who will tell you, "You should never do that.", "Who are you to think you could be the boss?" Share it only with people who will tell you, "Go for it!!!"

7. **Make lists.**

   Besides your list of goals you should spend 15 minutes a day on the following lists:

   a. What do I need to know and do to get to the goal?

   b. How could I sabotage my goals? Write down this list and throw it away every day, and spend more time on other lists.

   c. What will I commit myself to doing in the next day, week, month to fulfill my wants?

   d. What is the most important item on the list? Put the items in priority. Be sure to distinguish between what is "IMPORTANT" and what is "URGENT". Decide to do the "IMPORTANT" items first. They will help you reach your goal much quicker than if you concentrate only on what is "URGENT".

8. **Eliminate:**

   a. Criticism of self and others.
   b. Complaining about self or others (especially when you have no control over them, which is about 100% of the time.)

    c. Conflicting with others such as arguing or trying to convince them that you are right and they are wrong.

9. Develop mottos and slogans related to your goals.

    Look up the section in this book that contains sample slogans. You can use these or others. Repeat them aloud at home each morning. You will then start off the day on a positive note rather than with a tired, negative, self-defeating attitude.

10. Do all the above over and over again.

    If you don't have a plan for achieving your goals, spend more time and energy planting them in your mind. Do not become bogged down in why you cannot achieve the goals. Past failures are not important. There is one famous author who had over 700 rejections of manuscripts before he had one accepted by a publisher. He now has over 500 books in print!!!

HANG IN THERE!!

CHAPTER 10

MAKING YOURSELF ATTRACTIVE: AIDS TO MORE EFFECTIVE RELATIONSHIPS

All of the ideas contained below will help you build satisfying relationships with other people. And most of the steps can be done alone. Does this sound contradictory? Actually, it makes a great deal of sense. In this Chapter, I stress ways that you can make yourself an attractive person so that you can more easily form relationships. If you make an effort to implement these ideas, you will attract people to you because you will be an interesting, exciting, positive, upbeat kind of person. And, more importantly, you will reach out to others with less hesitancy.

These efforts must be:

SUSTAINED!

REPEATED!

PERFORMED OVER AND OVER!

CARRIED OUT WITHOUT GIVING UP!

In other words, the program I am describing is just that -- A PROGRAM. The activities cannot be done for one day only. They must be done over and over again!

1. Define what you want: Set goals.

This step has been discussed above.

And so, if you have listed your wants and goals, categorized them, there is only one more substep: Put them in priority. Decide which is the most important. List them according to rank. If getting a better job is more important than keeping the home clean, put "better job" above "clean house". This is your list. There is no way to do it that is better than your way. There is no right or wrong way to prioritize your list. And remember two guidelines:

    A. Be precise and exact when you make your list, and be convinced that this first step is crucial. There should be no rushing "to get on with it." Take your time in setting goals and defining wants.

    B. At this stage, don't worry about how you'll get to your goal. Your brain will figure out a method.

2. Develop a self-improvement plan.

If you develop your own SIP (Self Improvement Plan) you will have a range of behaviors designed to achieve your goals and wants. You will also reformulate and redefine your goals. But remember, the discovery of how you will achieve your goals will be a by-product of your program. It should not be the main focus.

Your SIP should have several components:

    A. Reading: If you are to be a

more interesting and attractive person, it is important to put interesting and positive ideas into your mind. And so turn off the TV and read. I suggest a visit to a book store. Go to the "Self-Improvement" section and find a book that appeals to you. There is a wealth of self-help literature in the bookstores and you will change your life for the better if you consistently read positive and inspirational literature. I recommend 15 minutes per day. At the end of this book, I've included a list of several books that will be helpful to you.

B. Doing: Another component of the SIP is to take on some activities that are uplifting. I suggest an exercise program. Of course, it should be realistic and a physician or health professional should be consulted if necessary. But 10 minutes of exercise each day, a brisk walk, or regular visits to the health spa, tennis court, or running track will help you feel success, be more creative, and gain in energy. In short, you will feel more proud of yourself and be more appealing to others. The reason you will be more attractive to others is not because of a beautiful body but because you will develop a beautiful mind.

C. Talking: More will be said about this step in the subsequent Pages. It is sufficient to say here: DON'T LAY YOUR TROUBLES ON OTHER PEOPLE. It's true that sometimes you need to let out the problems, and this is healthy. But don't do it indiscriminately! Pick a trusted friend, but don't abuse the friendship. And in the discussion, include your own ideas about what you are doing about your problems. Discuss possible solutions as the emphasis in any conversation about problems. The reverse is true too! When someone dumps their problems on you, listen politely for a while, then ask them such questions as:

"Can you work it out?"
"What could you do that would help the situation?"
"Do you have a way of handling it?"
"How do you take your mind off the problem for a while?"

You will be a person who is helpful when you not only listen in a kind way, but when you learn useful questions to ask a troubled friend.

3. Don't criticize yourself or others.

A. If you're down on yourself, stop giving yourself reasons for being "no good". You are good. There is no one on this planet exactly like you. You are unique. So look for the positive. When you say negative things about yourself, tell yourself at least two positive things. Refuse to tell yourself the bad things about yourself unless you are willing to speak positively to yourself. You might even write down positive things on paper. In my own counseling I frequently ask people to make lists of their own positive qualities. This is difficult for a highly self-critical person, but it is a way to provide balance to the inclination to put yourself down.

SUGGESTION: Every night write down 3 things you did during the day that you are proud of. Don't worry about how "great" or "small" they are.

If you are down on yourself and continually tell yourself "I can't", "I'm no good", "I'm inferior", etc., seek help from a counselor who will help you put other thoughts into your mind and who will help you plan for success. Even a few visits to a counselor can be helpful.

B. If you're down on others, look for positive things to say. If you criticize your children, for instance, spend time with them doing activities that are non-controversial. Spend 15 minutes a day doing things that require "no corrections" on your part. Walk with them, play a game that is fun for both of you, help them with a project. You will build a relationship with them and you will feel better about yourself. These suggestions are useful in any relationships. But the activity must have the qualities listed below:

1. It must take effort;
2. It must be done repeatedly -- not just one time;
3. It must be worthwhile -- not just "busy work".

Fun activities are worthwhile. These three requirements exclude TV watching.

If you . . .

WANT to be a more interesting person. . .
CRITICIZE yourself less. . .
BE MORE POSITIVE about yourself. . .
BE MORE POSITIVE about others. . .

TURN OFF THE TV

and follow all the suggestions contained in this book!!

C. If someone criticizes you, when someone puts you down, "gets on your case", or disapproves of you, there are several things you can do:

1. Say nothing; ignore them.
2. Tell them, "That's your opinion. I see it differently."

-60-

3. You could state more assertively "I'd rather you refrain from putting me down. It doesn't help."
4. Remind them: "I'll listen to a positive suggestion, but not a negative put-down."

Whatever you say, remember the injunction:

DON'T FIGHT FIRE WITH FIRE

FIGHT FIRE WITH WATER

In other words, don't become sarcastic when someone puts you down. Don't descend to the level of attack. Remain above the battle by stating what you'll do; "I'll listen...": by stating what you want; "a positive suggestion": or by describing how you look at the situation; "I look at it differently." But above all, don't argue. If you argue, you play into the hands of a criticizer. State clearly:

1. What you want;
2. How you view the situation;
3. What you will and will not do.

4. Change your Self-Talk if it is not working.

Suggestion: Take the time to write down on a piece of paper the "self-talk" you engage in. Self-talk is the statements you make to yourself about yourself. Do you ever use such self-defeating statements as:

"I've always been that way."

"I can't get along with. . ."
"I could never achieve that. . ."
"I hate doing this. . ."
"I've never liked math ... or science ... literature, etc."
"I've never liked people like that. . ."
"That guy makes me mad."
"Poor me. I've got it rough."
"Ain't it awful?"
"It's unfair."

Perhaps you tell yourself these or many other negative self-limiting statements. If you want to become a positive upbeat person who is attractive to others, who spontaneously reaches out to form friendships, I have a suggestion:

REPLACE THIS DESTRUCTIVE SELF TALK.

IT IS HOLDING YOU BACK!!!

Replace it with such statements as,

"I enjoy doing. . ."
"I can handle this situation."
"I have many opportunities."
"Life is great."
"I can; I will. I can; I will. I can; I will."
"I might be down but I'm getting up."
"I now get along with. . ."
"I can achieve that. . ."
"Today I can. . ."
"I now like math ... or science ... or literature."
"I'm full of energy."
"I am very friendly."

These statements are designed to give you belief in yourself. When you come to see yourself as more worthwhile, more worthy of success and friendship, it will be easy for you to develop relationships.

5. When you talk to people, ask them about themselves. More specifically:

   A. Ask about how they spend their time, their likes, and dislikes, the things they enjoy. Don't settle for an answer, "I like golf." Ask them what they like about it; what gives them satisfaction about golf; what it takes to be a good golfer. You are trying to enter their world, and to appreciate their uniqueness. When they sense a genuine interest in their world, they are more inclined to want to enter yours.

   B. Ask about their wants, their goals, their dreams. Ask them what they want financially, materially, intellectually, spiritually, physically. In other words, "pick their brains" about themselves. Don't overdo it to the extent of prying, but ask them, for instance, what they would like to achieve materially or spiritually. As I said above, don't come on too strong and don't be afraid to make small talk. Show a genuine interest in their goals and their behavior.

6. Be willing to compromise.

   After you have an initial relationship started, be willing to compromise. I'm not speaking of compromising morals or principles -- only neutral wants and behaviors.

   You will never get all of what you want and so be willing to settle for a part of it. You have very precise pictures in your mind of the "ideal" relationship. In the very likely event that you don't find this ideal relationship, be willing to settle for something less. As you live the daily drama of your life, make the decision that it is OK to give something in order to get something. If you want "chicken on Sunday" be willing "to eat fish on Saturday".

7. When you're down, do something!!

   I once had a graduate student tell me that her grandmother told her, "When you're depressed, clean your oven". There is wisdom in that advice. When you feel badly, take action. It doesn't matter what kind of action. Make a plan and follow it out. Do something you've been procrastinating. It doesn't matter why you are depressed. Set yourself up for a successful experience no matter how small. Write a letter you've been putting off, wash the car, clean the garage, shine your shoes, read a chapter in a good book, take a brisk walk, call a friend and try to cheer him/her up! In any event, remember:

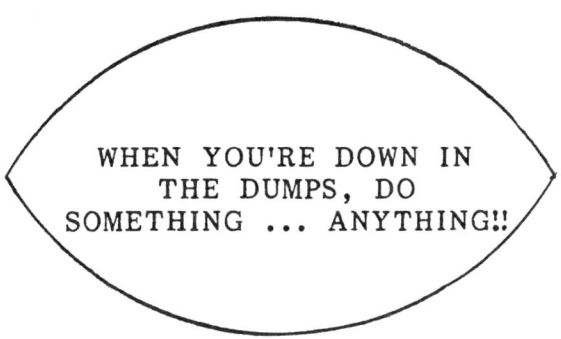

8. Remember that people always do the best they can!!! This goes for you and for others.

After you fail or make a mistake, remind yourself that you did the best you could at the time you did it. This is not easy to accept because of our tendency to be hard on ourselves and to criticize our efforts. But rather than put yourself down, just remind yourself that what you did in the past, at least seemed like a good idea, even though you might change your mind about it quickly. Sometime ago, I was driving on the expressway and thought it would be a good idea to pass the car in front of me. Almost immediately, I changed my mind when I saw the red light on the police car! Suddenly, it did not seem like a good idea! It takes only an instant to see that there is now a better way to do something.

The same is true of your friends. They always do things because they, at least, seem like good, if not the best, things to do. And so, look for the positive and point it out to them.

If you use the above 8 suggestions, you will

be able to build better relationships and form friendships. Most of the above activities can be done alone. To develop relationships you need not "force" yourself to meet people when you are uncomfortable with such behavior. If you are assertive and already feel comfortable in moving toward others, these ideas will enrich your relationships. If, on the other hand, you are more hesitant to extend yourself, you can still work on attaining the goal of being more friendly and involved by following the above suggestions. Be sure to pick from them without feeling you should adopt all of them at once. Work according to your level of power that you feel inside of you. But above all . . .

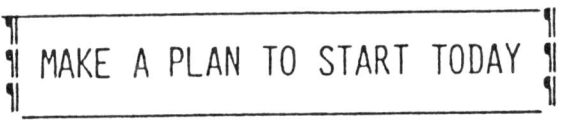

CHAPTER 11

A WORD ABOUT PLANNING

"Three frogs were sitting on a leaf. Two decided to jump. How many were left?"

Central to putting yourself together and keeping yourself in one piece is the need to continually make plans. Earlier, I referred to the axiom "To fail to plan is to plan to fail". Though it is important to define, clarify, and continually keep before you a clear set of wants and goals, still it is necessary to have a plan, a strategy, for getting what you want. It is not enough to <u>decide</u> to change. A plan must be formulated. In his book "<u>Be My Guest</u>", Conrad Hilton describes how he built his hotel empire.

"To accomplish big things, I am convinced you must first dream big dreams. True, it must be in line with progress, human and divine, or you are wasting your prayer. It has to be backed by work and faith, or it has no hands and feet. Maybe there's even an element of luck mixed in. But I am sure now that, without this master plan, you have nothing."

The essential ingredients are a dream (want, goal), a plan, and a faith or a belief in the value of your effort. The final chapter discusses faith and its role in achieving your goals. Though they are scattered throughout this book, I would like to bring together the necessary qualities of a successful plan.

In this way, you can post these next to

your wants on your bathroom mirror. (By now your entire mirror is probably covered). The plan should be a Samic^2/P or:

$$\frac{SAMIC^2}{P}$$

CHARACTERISTICS OF SUCCESSFUL PLANS:

Each letter stands for a characteristic of effective planning:

S = **Simple.** Don't make complicated plans in the beginning. And if you are a counselor who is using these ideas with clients, I'd suggest you teach them to cut through excuses and smoke screens by repeatedly asking them, "What's your plan for today, tonight, this week"?

A = **Attainable.** The plan should be a realistic one. The philosophy of Alcoholics Anonymous and Al-Anon, the self-help group for families of alcoholics, is reproduced below. It has worked for millions of people and has helped them live happy lives by adopting the "just for today" philosophy.

Just for today, I will live through this day only and not try to solve the whole problem of life at once.

Just for today, I will be unafraid of life and death, unafraid to enjoy the beautiful and be happy. Lincoln said, "Most people are as happy as they make up their minds to be".

Just for today, I will be agreeable, cheerful, charitable. I will praise people for what they do, not criticize them for what they cannot do. If I find fault, I will forgive and forget. I will not try to improve or regulate anybody except myself.

Just for today, I will look at life with fresh eyes and discover the wonder of it. I will know as I give to the world so the world will give to me.

Just for today, I will not show it if my feelings are hurt.

Just for today, I will find a little time to relax and realize what life is and can be. I will think about God and get a better perspective on myself.

M= Measurable. The tactics utilized to attain goals should be precise and exact. The most important question to ask is "when will I do it?" The time should be exact. "I'll do it tonight" is not a good plan. A person wishing to take a plane trip would not be satisfied if the travel agent said, "Your flight will leave tomorrow". A precise time is required by the potential traveler. So, too, the trip to better our mental health, serenity, higher achievement, and better relationshps requires exact planning.

I= **Immediate.** The plan should be executed as soon as possible, not "after vacation", "when the kids are out of school", "next month", or "later". Usually, at least some part of the plan can be implemented immediately.

C= **Controlled by the Planner.** The plan is not an "If Plan". It is not contingent upon whether someone else plans successfully. "I'll look for a job if someone wakes me" is not a good plan. The success of the plan should depend only upon the planner.

C= **Consistent.** The plan should be repeated over and over again. To attain a goal, the planner needs to repeat the plan on a consistent basis. Thus, to have a better relationship with a spouse or a child, it is not enough to take an annual vacation together. The quality time spent together should be planned on a regular basis.

P= **Persistence.** This is in some ways similar to the above characteristic - consistency. But, it also refers to a quality of the planner as a person. Many years ago, Napoleon Hill studied the characteristics of successful people to discover characteristics common to them. He found one quality which they all possessed: **PERSISTENCE,** or the ability to keep at it. This superceded genius, wealth, and any other quality.

The story is told of Winston Churchill, who in his old age was asked to give a talk to a high school

-70-

graduation class. He approached the microphone and gave a very brief speech, "Never, never, never give up."

The importance of persistence for long range results is also illustrated in the story of the Chinese bamboo tree, the Moso Tree. Each year, for 5 straight years, the Chinese farmer diligently waters the ground where the seeds were planted. For these 5 years, the seeds do not break the soil. There is no apparent result from this planting. Then, in the 6th year, the plant grows 90 feet in 6 weeks.

If the plan is SAMIC^2 over P or

$$\frac{SAMIC^2}{P}$$

you will prevail in your efforts to gain at least some control of your life.

Failed Plans:

The reader might say "you tell me to be persistent, to have faith in what I'm doing. What if my plans fail?" It is possible that not every plan or even many plans will get the desired result. I believe the best way to answer the question is in an indirect way. Consider the successes of the following people and their failures:

1. Babe Ruth held the record for home runs and strike-outs.

2. Willie Mays did not get a hit the first 26 times to the plate.

3. Barbara Gordon wrote I'm Dancing as Fast as I Can, her story of success over drugs and mental problems.

   She describes her deterioration, her depression, her drug dependency and her deepening sense of hopelessness. She also describes the way back, telling in detail her successful triumph over these problems and "failures". She now uses these failures to help thousands of people gain better control of their lives.

4. Thomas Edison invented the incandescent bulb. But he had many "failures" along the way. In fact, he tried 10,000 experiments before he succeeded. He was asked about how he felt to be right when he started. His answer, to the questioner, was that even though he had tried thousands of experiments that did not work, they were, nevertheless, successes. For he was thousands of steps closer in that he knew what did not work. He had 10,000 successes before he reached the one that was most successful.

5. Abraham Lincoln is one of the most outstanding examples of a person who failed on his way to success. Below is outlined the chronology of his success.

    '31 failed in business.
    '32 defeated for the legislature.
    '33 second failure in business.
    '36 nervous breakdown.
    '38 defeated for Speaker.

'40 defeated for elector.
'43 defeated for Congress.
'55 defeated for Senate.
'56 defeated for Vice-president.
1860 elected President of the United States.

In summary, all plans are, to some extent, successful, even if they don't work. To view your efforts this way might require a decision. Tell yourself, "I am going to make a plan, work at it. If it doesn't work, I'm one step closer to a plan that does work."

CHAPTER 12

THE ROLE OF FAITH

In order to succeeed, it helps to have what I choose to call Faith. For some, it is a belief in something outside themselves. For others, it is a belief in the efficiency of their plans, even though the result is much later, e.g., the Moso Tree. For others, it is a conviction that their work is meaningful, and purposeful, or contributory. For still others, it is a belief in all of the above along with an acceptance of the divine. Nevertheless, believing is a behavior that can penetrate our plans and give hope for the future. When a parent spends time with a child, there is a belief that this is an important act and has lasting value for the child.

If you are depressed, a plan to get active and involved with others is more likely to be satisfying if it is accompanied by the belief that such plans will ultimately have a salutary effect on how he/she feels.

The faith described above provides a bedrock for a superstructure of faith which some see as the ultimate reason for self-improvement. To change for the better connects us more intimately with all of creation.

We all seek to feel good and to be "self-actualized". Yet, there is another reason for personal growth.

It is my personal belief that as human beings, we all contain a spark of the divine. We are the "fingerprints" of the Almighty. Because of this vertical link, we are therefore linked horizontally on this earth, one with each other. The English poet, John Donne, described the human race as an island. When a small piece is washed away, the entire island is diminished. The French Theologian, Teilhard de Chardin, felt the human race is evolving toward a fullness of creation, a "pleroma", and when each of us evolves, "puts ourselves together", even in a microscopic way, we contribute actively to this journey toward the Divine.

Thus, when we change for the better, we truly change the world, we enhance it, we uplift it, we genuinely contribute in a permanent way, and we respond to the divine call to become everything we can be.

EPILOGUE

As stated in the beginning, this book is easy to read. It is a "how to" book intended for people who want to enrich their lives and are willing to do something to achieve that goal. The place to start is inside yourself. You won't succeed in making the world over to suit yourself, but you can make yourself over to be happy in this world. It means making a plan to take the kind of action described in this book. And so there is one final item to write, one further item to fill in.

I WILL TAKE BETTER COMMAND OF

MY OWN LIFE TODAY WITH THE

FOLLOWING PLANS:

1. _____

2. _____

3. _____

APPENDIX

Robert E. Wubbolding is an internationally known teacher, author and practitioner of Reality Therapy, and has taught the theory and practice of Reality Therapy in the United States, Europe, and Asia. He has written extensively on Reality Therapy including the widely acclaimed book Using Reality Therapy, Harper and Row, Publisher, 1988. He is currently writing two more books on Reality Therapy and he writes a regular column on Professional Issues for the Journal for Reality Therapy.

His busy professional life includes directing the training program of the CENTER FOR REALITY THERAPY and the CENTER FOR COUNSELING & MANAGING, a psychology practice devoted to the practice of Reality Therapy, as well as teaching counseling at Xavier University. His other duties include Senior Faculty and Board Member of the Institute of Reality Therapy in Los Angeles as well as chair of the Professional Development Committee in which he coordinates and monitors the Instructor Training Program of the Institute.

Formerly, he served as consultant to the drug and alcohol abuse programs of the US Army and Air Force. He was a group counselor at a Halfway House for Women, an Elementary and Secondary School Counselor, and a teacher of Adult Basic Education.

He is a Psychologist, a Licensed Professional Clinical Counselor and a member of many psychological and counseling organizations. He has received the Marvin Rammelsberg Award presented to a person in a helping profession who best exemplifies the qualities of friendship, brotherhood, and humanitarianism, and who displays exemplary leadership qualities and made outstanding contributions to professional organizations. He also received the Herman J. Peters award for exemplary leadership to promote the profession of counseling.

"**He is one of my closest and most trusted associates. I couldn't recommend anyone more highly."** Wm. Glasser, MD, Founder of Reality Therapy.

For more information on how to be trained in counseling, parenting, supervising and managing, contact:

ROBERT E. WUBBOLDING
CENTER FOR REALITY THERAPY
7777 MONTGOMERY RD.
CINCINNATI OHIO 45236

513-561-1911

LIST OF BOOKS

Buscaglia, Leo. Love. New York, Fawcett Crest, 1972.

Glasser, William. Control Theory. New York: Harper & Row, 1984. (Formerly published as Take Effective Control of your Life.

Glasser, William. Reality Therapy. New York: Harper& Row, 1965.

Leefeldt, Christine and Callenbach, Ernest. The Art of Friendship. New York: Berkeley Books, 1980.

Mandino, Og. The Greatest Salesman in the World. New York: Bantam Book, 1974.

Maltz, Maxwell. Psychocybernetics. New York, Pocket Books, 1969.

Ziglar, Zig. See You At The Top. Gretna: Pelican Publishing Company, 1981.